W9-BWD-607

WITHDRAWN

AMAZING TRAINS

Freight Trains

by Christina Leighton

BELLWETHER MEDIA · MINNEAPOLIS, MN

Note to Librarians, Teachers, and Parents:

Blastoff! Readers are carefully developed by literacy experts and combine standards-based content with developmentally appropriate text.

Level 1 provides the most support through repetition of high-frequency words, light text, predictable sentence patterns, and strong visual support.

Level 2 offers early readers a bit more challenge through varied simple sentences, increased text load, and less repetition of high-frequency words.

Level 3 advances early-fluent readers toward fluency through increased text and concept load, less reliance on visuals, longer sentences, and more literary language.

Level 4 builds reading stamina by providing more text per page, increased use of punctuation, greater variation in sentence patterns, and increasingly challenging vocabulary.

Level 5 encourages children to move from "learning to read" to "reading to learn" by providing even more text, varied writing styles, and less familiar topics.

Whichever book is right for your reader, Blastoff! Readers are the perfect books to build confidence and encourage a love of reading that will last a lifetime!

This edition first published in 2018 by Bellwether Media, Inc.

No part of this publication may be reproduced in whole or in part without written permission of the publisher. For information regarding permission, write to Bellwether Media, Inc., Attention: Permissions Department, 5357 Penn Avenue South, Minneapolis, MN 55419.

Library of Congress Cataloging-in-Publication Data

Names: Leighton, Christina, author.
Title: Freight Trains / by Christina Leighton.
Description: Minneapolis, MN : Bellwether Media, Inc., [2018] | Series:
  Blastoff! Readers: Amazing Trains | Includes bibliographical references
  and index. | Audience: Age 5-8. | Audience: Grade K to 3.
Identifiers: LCCN 2016052933 (print) | LCCN 2017010227 (ebook) | ISBN
  9781626176706 (hardcover : alk. paper) | ISBN 9781681034003 (ebook)
Subjects: LCSH: Railroad trains–Juvenile literature.
Classification: LCC TF148 .L45 2018 (print) | LCC TF148 (ebook) | DDC
  625.2–dc23
LC record available at https://lccn.loc.gov/2016052933

Editor: Nathan Sommer   Designer: Jon Eppard

Printed in the United States of America, North Mankato, MN.

Table of Contents

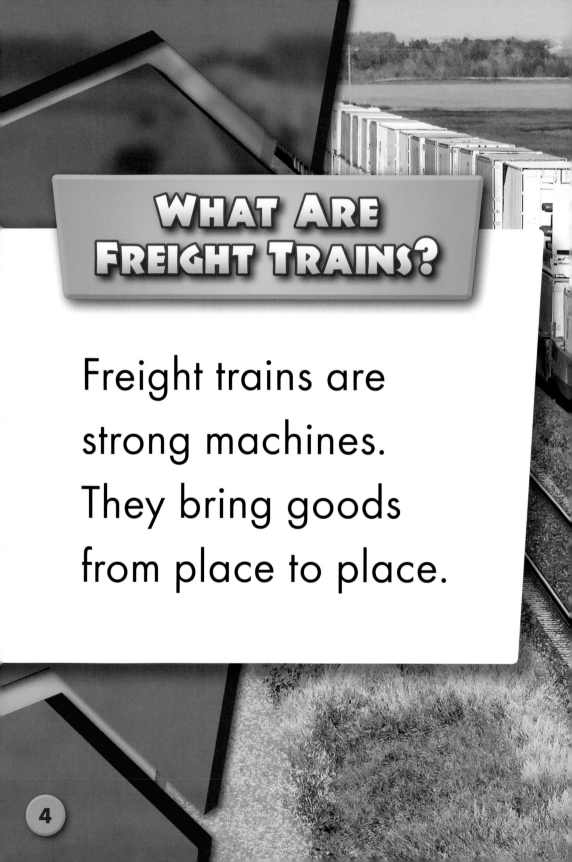

WHAT ARE FREIGHT TRAINS?

Freight trains are strong machines. They bring goods from place to place.

These trains carry many different types of **cargo**. They hold tons of weight.

cargo

Locomotives pull freight trains. Some trains need up to eight locomotives!

locomotive

Cars make up freight trains. There are many types of freight cars.

TONS OF WEIGHT

A freight car can hold around 200,000 pounds (90,718 kilograms). That is about the weight of 15 African elephants!

cars

Boxcars often move animals and frozen food. Flatcars can carry wood and machines.

flatcar

13

Open-top cars
often move **coal**
or seeds. Tank cars
carry **liquids**.

open-top cars

tank cars

PULLING AHEAD

Engineers control freight trains. They get cargo to where it needs to be.

engineer →

Freight trains cross the country. They travel hundreds of miles.

Their heavy loads shake the ground! What is this freight train carrying?

Glossary

cargo

goods carried by
a train

engineers

train drivers

cars

vehicles pulled by
a train

liquids

substances that flow
freely like water

coal

a hard black substance
that is burned for fuel

locomotives

vehicles with engines
that pull train cars

To Learn More

AT THE LIBRARY
Clapper, Nikki Bruno. *Freight Trains*. North Mankato, Minn.: Capstone Press, 2016.

Klein, Adria F. *Freight Train*. North Mankato, Minn.: Stone Arch Books, 2013.

Richardson, Adele D. *Freight Trains in Action*. Mankato, Minn.: Capstone Press, 2012.

ON THE WEB
Learning more about freight trains is as easy as 1, 2, 3.

1. Go to www.factsurfer.com.

2. Enter "freight trains" into the search box.

3. Click the "Surf" button and you will see a list of related web sites.

With factsurfer.com, finding more information is just a click away.

Index

The images in this book are reproduced through the courtesy of: Serjio74, front cover; Scanrail1, pp. 2-3;
Steve Boyko, pp. 4-5; Mayskyphoto, pp. 6-7, 18-19; StonePhotos, pp. 8-9, 22 (bottom right); trainman111,
pp. 10-11; tristan tan, p. 11 (elephants); PILart, p. 11 (freight car); Taina Sohlman, pp. 12-13, 22 (top left);
LeksusTuss, pp. 14-15; Jim West/ Alamy, pp. 16-17, 22 (top right); BeyondImages, pp. 20-21; A. and I. Kruk,
p. 22 (center left); kubais, p. 22 (center right); Brad Sauter, p. 22 (bottom left).